William Springborn

Step 1

The Foundation Of Recovery

Revised Edition

HAZELDEN

Hazelden
Center City, Minnesota 55012-0176

ISBN: 0-89486-017-8

We admitted we were powerless over alcohol—that our lives had become unmanageable.

—STEP ONE

This pamphlet aims to drive home one point: To become clean and sober, we've got to understand Step One of Alcoholics Anonymous (AA).

Alcohol and other drugs are chemicals that alter our moods. For that reason, I use the words *alcoholism* and *chemical dependency* to mean the same thing. The same is true of *alcoholic* and *chemically dependent.*

—WILLIAM S.

Life is bigger than any of us. *Powerlessness* and *unmanageability*, mentioned in Step One, are big words that point to a simple fact: When some of us use drugs or alcohol, life spirals out of control. We can't stop using, even when we want to. And when we start using, we lose control over how much we use and how we act.

All this can be hard to accept at first. Just keep one thing in mind as you read what follows: The purpose of Step One is not to label us or put us down. The real purpose is to help us learn new ways of thinking, feeling, and acting. When we learn these things, we become much more comfortable with ourselves and others. Life starts to work again—better than ever before.

Taking Step One is also easier when we remember something else: We cannot control how any situation turns out. We are responsible only for the effort we put forth.

I invite you to join me in the marvelous experience of becoming sober and clean. The Twelve Steps of AA have led millions to this experience. And it all starts with telling the truth about where we are— right now, today. Just begin with two words: *powerlessness* and *unmanageability*.

SERENITY TO ACCEPT THE THINGS I CANNOT CHANGE.

*We admitted we were powerless over
alcohol . . .*

Most of us started using alcohol or drugs for many
of the same reasons:

- to relax
- to have fun
- to be part of a group
- to be accepted
- to be successful

Chances are, not one of us started using chemicals
with the idea of getting addicted. But then our problems started mounting. In response, many of us said
or thought things like these:

- "If I can discover the problem areas in my life,
  I'll be okay."
- "My only problem is my job; I'm not getting
  promoted fast enough."
- "I can't get along with my boss."
- "My mate is too demanding, too critical."
- "My family just doesn't understand me."
- "I live in a bad neighborhood; it's the neighbors'
  fault."
- "All I have to do is understand myself—why I
  let things bother me—and my drinking will get
  under control."

Do any of these sound familiar? With such attitudes, we fail to see what's really happening in our lives.

A look at how our bodies react to chemicals

People with chemical dependency have something we can call an *X-factor*. This means that they respond to alcohol and other drugs in an unusual way.

Many people get high when they use drugs or alcohol. But they can stop using if they feel sick or if using leads to problems. This is not true for chemically dependent people. Drinking or using drugs makes us feel great. And once we start using, we can't stop even when we want to.

Experts think this happens because our bodies react to drugs and alcohol in a unique way. We call it the X-factor because no one knows exactly why this is true. Many studies have been made of this problem. But so far, no one can explain why some people become chemically dependent and others do not.

The main point is that *we are not responsible for the X-factor*. Think of it this way: Some of us have blue eyes and some of us have brown eyes. Some of us have a heart condition or diabetes, and some of us don't. Likewise, some people who use drugs and alcohol will get addicted to them, and others will not.

People who have blue eyes or diabetes are not bad people. They are not weak-willed or lazy. Their bodies are just different from the rest of ours. In the same way, those of us with the X-factor are not bad, weak-willed, or lazy. Our bodies just respond to alcohol and drugs in a different way.

We can call the X-factor *physical powerlessness*. This means that we can't control how our bodies react to alcohol and drugs. We don't have to feel bad or guilty about that. The X-factor is just a disease we share. It's simply a fact of our existence!

So our bodies can get addicted to drugs and alcohol. But chemical dependency is a disease of the mind as well as the body. Let's look more closely at how our minds work.

A look at how we think about chemicals

Experts say that we have a psychological as well as a physical dependency on alcohol and other drugs. We've looked at physical powerlessness. But what does *psychological powerlessness* mean?

As chemically dependent people, we have an urge to use our chemical of choice. That urge rules our lives. In fact, the urge to get high again is so strong that we forsake many—or even all—of our values. We throw away what's most important to us: families, jobs, personal welfare, respect, and integrity. We do all this just to satisfy the urge to get high. We remember the good times we had during the early stages of our drinking, and we want to repeat them no matter what the cost.

Once this urge exists, it takes on a life of its own. We may not think of drinking or getting stoned all the time, or even every day. Still, the urge is just below the surface, ready to rise again. And even though we are not aware of it, the urge can start ruling our lives at any time.

We don't understand why this happens to our minds, any more than we understand how the X-factor happens to our bodies. Again, it's just that we have a physical and mental disease. This further shows how powerless we are over drugs and alcohol.

If you read *Alcoholics Anonymous* (also called the Big Book), you'll see it expressed this way:

> We know that while the alcoholic keeps away from drink, as he may do for months or years, he reacts much like other men. We are equally positive that once he takes any alcohol whatever into his system, something happens, both in the bodily and mental sense, which makes it virtually impossible for him to stop. . . .
>
> And the truth, strange to say, is usually that he has no more idea why he took that first drink than you have. Some drinkers have excuses with which they are satisfied part of the time. But in their hearts they really do not know why they do it. Once this malady has a real hold, they are a baffled lot.*

The stresses and strains of daily life—hangovers, family problems, job hassles, and many more—are more evidence that we're powerless. Such problems are noted on the chart that follows (pages 8-9).

---

*Alcoholics Anonymous [The Big Book], 3d ed. (New York: AA World Services, Inc., 1976), 22-23.

Addictic

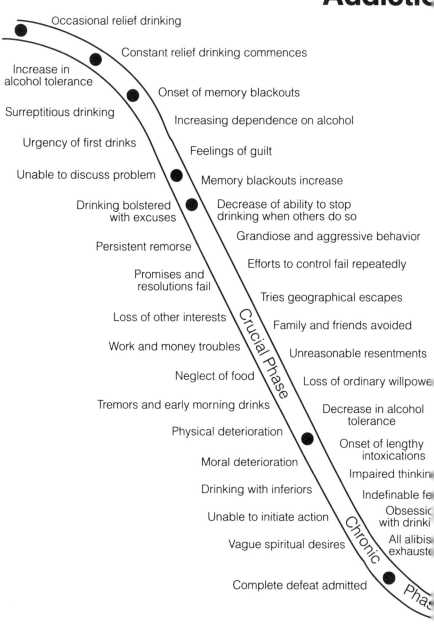

Occasional relief drinking

Constant relief drinking commences

Increase in alcohol tolerance

Onset of memory blackouts

Surreptitious drinking

Increasing dependence on alcohol

Urgency of first drinks

Feelings of guilt

Unable to discuss problem

Memory blackouts increase

Drinking bolstered with excuses

Decrease of ability to stop drinking when others do so

Grandiose and aggressive behavior

Persistent remorse

Efforts to control fail repeatedly

Promises and resolutions fail

Tries geographical escapes

Loss of other interests

Family and friends avoided

Work and money troubles

Unreasonable resentments

Neglect of food

Loss of ordinary willpowe

Crucial Phase

Tremors and early morning drinks

Decrease in alcohol tolerance

Physical deterioration

Onset of lengthy intoxications

Moral deterioration

Impaired thinkin

Drinking with inferiors

Indefinable fe

Unable to initiate action

Obsessic with drinki

Vague spiritual desires

All alibis exhauste

Chronic

Complete defeat admitted

Phas

Obsessive drinking con in vicious circles

d Recovery

Enlightened and interesting way of
life opens up with road ahead to
higher levels than ever before

Group therapy and
mutual help continue

Increasing tolerance

Rationalizations recognized

Contentment in sobriety

Care of personal appearance

First steps toward
economic stability

Confidence of employers

Increase of emotional control

Application of real values

Facts faced with courage

Rebirth of ideals

New circle of stable friends

New interests develop

Family and friends
appreciate efforts

Adjustment to family needs

Natural rest and sleep

Realistic thinking

Desire to escape goes

Return of self-esteem

Regular nourishment
taken

Diminishing fears
of the unknown
future

Appreciation of possibilities
of new way of life

Start of group therapy

Onset of new hope

Physical overhaul by doctor

tual needs examined

Right thinking begins

sisted in making
rsonal stocktaking

Meets former addicts normal and happy

s taking alcohol

Learns
coholism is
an illness

Told addiction can be arrested

Honest desire for help

Rehabilitation

An honest look at the first half of this chart will help us understand powerlessness. Then we'll start to get past our self-deception and the fear that surrounds our chemical use.

How it all adds up

Physical powerlessness means we can't use drugs or alcohol like other people. Psychological powerlessness means we can't quit once we start using. In short, *we can't use and we can't quit.* We're at the end of our rope. If we continue on this path, we'll die or be driven insane from our disease. That's powerlessness.

Chemical dependency is progressive. That means it can get steadily worse over time. And if it is not arrested, it will destroy us totally—not only physically and emotionally, but spiritually as well.

Even after looking honestly at their own lives, some people have doubts about admitting powerlessness. The Big Book has some advice for them: "Step over to the nearest barroom and try some controlled drinking. Try to drink and stop abruptly."* Few of us really have to go through with this. We already know what the results would be.

Get past the barriers to admitting powerlessness

The founders of AA saw how important it is for us to admit powerlessness. That's why they made this admission the first part of Step One.

It is not easy to admit powerlessness over anything. Many of us would rather not face this at all. We don't want to see how our drinking or drug use hurts and upsets other people. This is as much a

---

*Alcoholics Anonymous, 31.

symptom of our illness as liver damage, withdrawal, or digestive disorder. According to page 60 of the Big Book, "Those who do not recover are people who cannot or will not completely give themselves to this simple program, usually men and women who are constitutionally incapable of being honest with themselves."

We often tell ourselves and others: "But I don't need to drink. I don't drink all the time." Saying this is buying into a myth: *All I need to control a drinking or drug problem is willpower.* That myth can make us unwilling to study our powerlessness.

Another barrier to admitting powerlessness is imitating certain social ideals. We try to be a macho man or sophisticated lady. We try to avoid the labels "dope fiend" or "drug addict." Negative attitudes toward addicts are changing, and more people accept that addiction is a disease. But the change is coming slowly. Many in our society still think of drug addicts as the lowest forms of chemically dependent people. We often hear the families of dependent people say: *Thank God it's only a drinking problem and not drug addiction.*

Page 20 of the Big Book lists some other phrases we'll hear:

- "Lay off the hard stuff."
- "Why don't you try beer and wine?"
- "His willpower must be weak."
- "He could stop if he wanted to."

These ideas make it harder for people to get help. They end up seeking help only after family discord, job difficulties, loss of self-respect, or some other crisis.

11

As we continue in sobriety, we understand more deeply how to live with chemical dependency. We see that getting this disease is *not* our personal responsibility. At the same time, we *are* personally responsible for doing what it takes to begin recovery.

Admit powerlessness—regain yourself

Admitting powerlessness is a way to freedom. We release ourselves from the insanity, the morning shakes, the loss of respect. We regain interest in what's important to us. We stop the physical abuse that alcohol and other drugs heap on our nervous system. We stop our liver and other vital organs from deteriorating even more. And we shake up faulty thinking—the lies we've told so many times that we've started to believe them ourselves. We stop losing moral ground, and we start to win back our individual values.

Ask yourself: *When I admit powerlessness, what am I really giving up?* All you're really giving up is misery, pain, discomfort, and settling for mere existence.

Build on firm ground

Accepting powerlessness is like laying the foundation of a building. Before a building can stand, the foundation has to be solid. When we thoroughly admit our own powerlessness, we lay a solid foundation for recovery.

Many times we see people taking powerlessness for granted or treating it with a casual attitude. *Understanding powerlessness must be the foundation for any successful recovery from chemical dependency.* Stressing powerlessness does not mean we forget the rest of the Twelve Steps. It only means we're putting recovery on firm footing.

As we begin to truly understand chemical dependency, we also begin to understand our personal powerlessness. We are not ashamed to admit that we're powerless over this disease, just as we are powerless over any other disease. We also learn that survival comes only through a total program of recovery. People with diabetes or heart disease have an ongoing program to keep their health in check. For chemical dependency we need the same strategy.

Personal responsibility for any disease occurs when we admit and accept that we have the symptoms. Then it's our job to start a recovery program. At this point, condemning ourselves for being chemically dependent is self-defeating. Remorse and guilt only lead to more defeat.

Unlock old patterns

When we stop using chemicals, we do not solve the problem. Fear of physical withdrawal and meeting life without our "crutch" has led us to stay drunk or stoned for a long time. In the process, we learned attitudes that keep us locked in rigid behaviors.

Reading page 30 of the Big Book helps us unlock those patterns:

> We learned that we had to fully concede to our innermost selves that we were alcoholics. This is the first step in recovery. The delusion that we are like other people, or presently may be, has to be smashed.
>
> We alcoholics are men and women who have lost the ability to control our drinking. We know that no real alcoholic *ever* recovers control.

Find an atmosphere of caring and concern

Admitting powerlessness often leads to emotional pain, and chemically dependent people seem to have a low threshold for pain. That makes it crucial for us to find care, concern, and reinforcement in AA and treatment programs.

Chemically dependent people walk a tightrope. In recovery, we see how precarious our situation really is. Others can help us see the painful side of our alcohol and chemical use. At the same time, we need emotional support as we work through all this. Only then can we accept our disease gracefully.

Look at your own powerlessness

Honestly answering the following questions will help you prove and accept, on a gut level, your individual powerlessness. If you need more room, feel free to continue on a separate sheet. Review your answers with your sponsor.

1. List three things that you did when using alcohol or other drugs—things that you would not do when sober.

   1.

   2.

   3.

2. List three ways you violated your own value system when using alcohol or other drugs.

   1.

   2.

   3.

3. List three personality changes that occurred in you when you were using alcohol or other drugs.

   1.

   2.

   3.

4. List three times you tried to quit and resumed using.

    1.

    2.

    3.

5. Describe three times when you physically hurt yourself or others as a result of using.

    1.

    2.

    3.

6. List other examples of how powerlessness (loss of control) has revealed itself in your own personal experience.

7. How has your body been hurt by your disease?

8. Give three examples of personality traits that block you from admitting powerlessness.

    1.

    2.

    3.

9. What convinces you that you no longer can use alcohol or drugs safely?

10. Are you an alcoholic or chemically dependent person?

Your notes:

_____

_____

_____

_____

_____

_____

_____

_____

_____

_____

_____

_____

_____

_____

_____

. . . that our lives had become
unmanageable.

If we want to recover, we must understand personal powerlessness. What helps us most is taking an honest look at how drinking or using drugs has affected us. Instead of living as free and natural people, we were reduced to fighting for survival. That's unmanageability.

Unmanageability is tied to powerlessness. Many types of social pressures and stress prevent us from directing our own lives. That leads to two kinds of unmanageability: social and personal.

Social unmanageability

Social unmanageability follows directly from taking alcohol or other mood-altering drugs. There is little doubt that an intoxicated person driving an automobile is unmanageable. People who are filled with amphetamines and pushing their bodies beyond the point of exhaustion are unmanageable. We see social unmanageability in DWIs, arrests for disorderly conduct, family arguments, or fights after intoxication. People under the influence of any drug will react in a drug-induced way. Addiction directly affects our emotions and our behavior—in fact, every area of our lives.

This behavior is not unique to chemically dependent people. Almost any person who consumed alcohol or other drugs in the quantities that we have would be out of control.

Often we can find unmanageable behavior in our pasts. Think back to family gatherings or office parties. Some of us had "one too many" and became more boisterous than normal. Perhaps we told off-color stories. Perhaps we danced or related to the opposite sex in a way that's unusual for us. At our jobs, chemical use led to lost hours and shirked responsibilities. In any case, we can now see that we were unmanageable.

Personal unmanageability

Personal unmanageability involves attitudes and beliefs about ourselves, our environment, and the people we live with. In many cases, personal unmanageability was present many years before chemical addiction.

It's widely believed that alcohol or pills are the "demons" in our lives. Actually, it is ourselves, not the pills or alcohol, that cause most of our problems. Chemicals can destroy a person only if that person learns how to justify chemical abuse.

According to AA, putting the cork in the bottle is not enough. We need to rejuvenate our personalities. We have to learn about ourselves on an intimate level. We have to discover what AA calls our "character defects" and "shortcomings." As we do, we learn to accept ourselves as human beings with strong and weak points just like everyone else.

Chemically dependent people seem to have some defects in common. One is *self-centeredness.* In fact, this defect has to be present for our disease to prosper. Selfishness may call for a direct assault to break out of our denial system, rebuild trust, and regain concern for other people.

Another defect is the fundamental *immaturity* that seems to be prevalent among chemically dependent people. Immaturity causes us to respond to life in a self-defeating way. Immature behavior can also occur when we are sober, and it may not be obvious. Some people, for instance, function well when sober. But when they feel even a little agitated or find their normal patterns disrupted, they react in extremes.

Overreacting is definitely immature. In fact, any behavior that lowers our self-respect or dignity is immature. Some examples are temper tantrums, failing to share feelings honestly, and insisting on having our own way. Such patterns can expand and gradually take over our personalities.

Because people are all so different, personal unmanageability covers a wide range of behaviors. We do, however, share some basic desires. We want to love and be loved. We want to feel worthwhile. The point is this: Fulfilling these desires is much easier when we meet life on life's terms. That's better than the constant battle to mold life according to our own demands.

Look at your own unmanageability

Honestly answering the following questions will help you prove and accept, on a gut level, your individual unmanageability. If you need more room, feel free to continue on a separate sheet. Review your answers with your sponsor.

1. What does unmanageability mean to you?

2. List three incidents that took place while you were using—incidents that led you to feel shame.

   1.

   2.

   3.

3. Give examples of your behaviors when you tried to "quit without a program."

4. On this and the next page, give three examples of how your alcohol or drug use has interfered with your personal goals.

   1.

2.

3.

5. Give three examples of feelings you tried to alter by using chemicals.

    1.

    2.

    3.

6. Give three examples of healthier ways you've learned to deal with your feelings.

    1.

    2.

3.

7. Chances are that some crisis brought you to recovery. What crisis besides this one would have eventually happened if you'd kept using chemicals?

8. What changes in your life do you hope to make in sobriety? (For help, read the promises listed in the Big Book on pages 83 and 84.)

9. Write six personal promises you hope to keep in recovery.

    1.

    2.

3.

4.

5.

6.

Your notes:

_____
_____
_____
_____
_____
_____
_____
_____
_____

If you forget Step One, will you remember how to stay clean and sober?

Admitting powerlessness and unmanageability is not pleasant. We need courage and willingness to face up to what the disease actually has done to us. Looking honestly at how sick we've become can give us the push to move on, to accept the stark reality about ourselves, our disease, and what it takes to get well.

If people told you this would be easy, they lied. But on the other hand, people can live this program. If they couldn't, they wouldn't survive. Surviving this disease is as hard as we want to make it.

So love yourself enough to admit that you're powerless over your chemical of choice—that your life is unmanageable. You already know the results of your old way of life. What you don't fully see is the promise that recovery holds for you. Join us!

The Twelve Steps of Alcoholics Anonymous[*]

1. We admitted we were powerless over alcohol—that our lives had become unmanageable.

2. Came to believe that a Power greater than ourselves could restore us to sanity.

3. Made a decision to turn our will and our lives over to the care of God *as we understood Him.*

4. Made a searching and fearless moral inventory of ourselves.

5. Admitted to God, to ourselves, and to another human being the exact nature of our wrongs.

6. Were entirely ready to have God remove all these defects of character.

7. Humbly asked Him to remove our shortcomings.

8. Made a list of all persons we had harmed, and became willing to make amends to them all.

9. Made direct amends to such people wherever possible, except when to do so would injure them or others.

10. Continued to take personal inventory and when we were wrong promptly admitted it.

11. Sought through prayer and meditation to improve our conscious contact with God *as we understood Him,* praying only for knowledge of His will for us and the power to carry that out.

12. Having had a spiritual awakening as the result of these steps, we tried to carry this message to alcoholics, and to practice these principles in all our affairs.

---

[*]The Twelve Steps of AA are taken from *Alcoholics Anonymous,* 3d ed., published by AA World Services, Inc., New York, N.Y., 59-60. Reprinted with permission of AA World Services, Inc. (See editor's note on the copyright page.)

HAZELDEN CLASSIC STEP PAMPHLETS

Step One: *The Foundation of Recovery*
#1425

Step Two: *Coming to Believe*
#1273

Step Three: *Making a Decision*
#1277

Step Four: *Getting Honest*
#1286

Step Five: *Telling My Story*
#1281

Steps Six and Seven: *Ready, Willing, and Able*
#1287

Step Eight: *Preparing for Change*
#1288

Step Nine: *Repairing the Past*
#1289

Step Ten: *Maintaining My New Life*
#1294

Step Eleven: *Partnership with a Higher Power*
#1431

Step Twelve: *Carrying the Message*
#1301

4—

www.hazelden.org

15251 Pleasant Valley Road
P.O. Box 176
Center City, MN 55012-0176

1-800-328-9000 (Toll Free U.S. and Canada)
1-651-213-4000 (Outside the U.S. and Canada)
1-651-213-4590 (Fax)

Order No. 1425

ISBN 978-0-89486-017-
9000

9 780894 860171